Praise for
SUPER SCRATCH
PROGRAMMING ADVENTURE!

"Reveals the power of this deceptively simple programming language . . . A fun way to learn how to program Scratch, even for adults."
—Mark Frauenfelder, Boing Boing

"A great introduction to game design. Kids will start building games from the first page."
—Liz Upton, The Raspberry Pi Project

"If you think you might have a future programmer on your hands, it's time to introduce your kid to Scratch. . . . *Super Scratch Programming Adventure!* makes it even easier to get started."
—Ruth Suehle, *GeekMom*

"If you have a kid who plays around with a computer and can read even a little, get this."
—Greg Laden, *National Geographic*'s *ScienceBlogs*

"An enjoyable and highly accessible introduction to this technology and the power of computing."
—Patrice Gans, *Education Week*'s *BookMarks*

"If you've got a child or maybe even a classroom of students who are wanting to make their own games, Scratch is a great option. . . . For structured training that is also entertaining, *Super Scratch Programming Adventure!* will make a great textbook."
—James Floyd Kelly, *GeekDad*

"Walks readers through a series of extremely well-designed game-design projects, each of which introduces a new concept or two to young programmers, providing a gentle learning curve for mastering Scratch's many powerful features."
—Cory Doctorow, Boing Boing

"If you're looking for a way to get your kid interested in programming, and Scratch in particular, I can't recommend this Scratch book enough."
—Chris O'Brien, *San Jose Mercury News*' *SiliconBeat*

SUPER SCRATCH PROGRAMMING ADVENTURE!

LEARN TO PROGRAM BY MAKING COOL GAMES!

THE LEAD PROJECT

no starch press

Super Scratch Programming Adventure! Copyright © 2019 by the LEAD Project. This edition has been updated to cover Scratch 3.

Super Scratch Programming Adventure! is a translation of the original Traditional Chinese–language edition, *Easy LEAD* 創意程式設計 *Scratch* 遊俠傳 (*Easy LEAD: The Scratch Musketeers*), ISBN 978-988-18408-2-0, published by the Hong Kong Federation of Youth Groups, © 2010 by the Hong Kong Federation of Youth Groups.

All rights reserved. No part of this work may be reproduced or transmitted in any form or by any means, electronic or mechanical, including photocopying, recording, or by any information storage or retrieval system, without the prior written permission of the copyright owner and the publisher.

Printed in Korea

First printing

23 22 21 20 19   1 2 3 4 5 6 7 8 9

ISBN-10: 1-7185-0012-2
ISBN-13: 978-1-71850-012-9

Publisher: William Pollock
Adviser: Dr. Rosanna Wong Yick-ming, DBE, JP
Editorial Team: Yolanda Chiu, Alice Lui, Edmond Kim Ping Hui
Contributors: Edmond Kim Ping Hui (Book Contents); Man Chun Chow, Chun Hei Tse,
      Vincent Wong (Assistance & Photography)
Interior Design: LOL Design Ltd.
Production Editors: Serena Yang and Meg Sneeringer
Cover Design: Tina Salameh
Developmental Editors: Tyler Ortman, Alex Freed, and Annie Choi
Technical Reviewers: Michael Smith-Welch and Martin Tan
Compositors: Laurel Chun, Riley Hoffman, and Kim Scott/Bumpy Design
Proofreaders: Alison Law and Kassie Andreadis

For information on distribution, translations, or bulk sales,
please contact No Starch Press, Inc. directly:

No Starch Press, Inc.
245 8th Street, San Francisco, CA 94103
phone: 415.863.9900; info@nostarch.com; http://www.nostarch.com/

Library of Congress Cataloging-in-Publication Data
A catalog record of the first edition of this book is available from the Library of Congress.

No Starch Press and the No Starch Press logo are registered trademarks of No Starch Press, Inc. Other product and company names mentioned herein may be the trademarks of their respective owners. Rather than use a trademark symbol with every occurrence of a trademarked name, we are using the names only in an editorial fashion and to the benefit of the trademark owner, with no intention of infringement of the trademark.

The information in this book is distributed on an "As Is" basis, without warranty. While every precaution has been taken in the preparation of this work, neither the author nor No Starch Press, Inc. shall have any liability to any person or entity with respect to any loss or damage caused or alleged to be caused directly or indirectly by the information contained in it.

All characters in this publication are fictitious, and any resemblance to real persons, living or dead, is purely coincidental.

CONTENTS

FOREWORD BY PROFESSOR MITCHEL RESNICK — 8

A NOTE OF THANKS FROM DR. ROSANNA WONG YICK-MING — 9

A NOTE FOR PARENTS AND EDUCATORS — 10

MEET THE CAST — 18

STAGE 1: RIDING A FLARE FROM THE SUN — 19
Let's get to know Scratch! We'll also learn about sprites and coordinates.

STAGE 2: ENTERING SPACE — 31
This is where you'll make your first game. You'll also learn how to create new costumes and program a sprite's movements, reactions, and sound effects.

STAGE 3: TRAPPED BY MONA LISA'S SMILE — 51
While writing this two-part game, you'll learn how to control the flow of a Scratch project. You'll see how to keep score using variables and control the order of the game using broadcasts.

STAGE 4: DEFEND HONG KONG'S TECHNOCORE — 61
You'll learn to control sprites with the mouse, program objects to bounce back, and more.

STAGE 5: PENALTY KICK IN IPANEMA — 71
You'll program a soccer game with a targeting system, several related rules, interactive sound effects, and a vivid, animated background!

STAGE 6: SCRATCHY'S WILD RIDE 85
You'll learn how to create a side-scrolling racing game, program complex movements for sprites, and make the game's background change over time.

STAGE 7: THE LOST TREASURES OF GIZA 105
In this Egyptian adventure, you'll create an interactive maze with a guard, booby traps, and treasure!

STAGE 8: WIZARD'S RACE! 119
When you make this simple button-mashing game, you'll also learn how to play music with Scratch and create an animated background.

STAGE 9: THE FINAL FIGHT...IN DARK SPACE 131
You'll need to use all the knowledge you've gained while making this exciting fighting game. You'll create two characters with unique fight moves, custom health counters, and more.

STAGE 10: EPILOGUE 151

CLOSING THOUGHTS FROM EDMOND KIM PING HUI 155

ONLINE RESOURCES 156

FOREWORD

Scratch is more than a piece of software. It is part of a broader educational mission. We designed Scratch to help young people prepare for life in today's fast-changing society. As young people create Scratch projects, they are not just learning how to write computer programs. They are learning to think creatively, reason systematically, and work collaboratively—essential skills for success and happiness in today's world.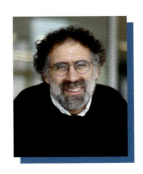

It has been exciting to see all of the creative ways that young people are using Scratch. On the Scratch website (*http://scratch.mit.edu/*), young people from around the world are sharing a wide variety of creative projects: animated stories, adventure games, interactive tutorials, guided tours, science experiments, online newsletters, and much more. Scratch is a digital sandbox where young people can express themselves creatively—and, in the process, develop as creative thinkers.

Super Scratch Programming Adventure! will help introduce more young people to the creative possibilities of Scratch. The book grows out of one of the world's most innovative and productive Scratch initiatives, organized by the Hong Kong Federation of Youth Groups. I'm delighted that their ideas and activities are now available to teachers, parents, and children around the world.

As you read this book, let your imagination run wild. What will you create with Scratch?

Enjoy the adventure!

Professor Mitchel Resnick
Director, MIT Scratch Team
MIT Media Lab

A NOTE OF THANKS

The Hong Kong Federation of Youth Groups created the Learning through Engineering, Art and Design (LEAD) Project in 2005 in collaboration with the MIT Media Lab and the Chinese University of Hong Kong. The LEAD Project promotes hands-on, design-based activities with the creative use of technology and aims to develop an innovative spirit among the youth of Hong Kong. Since its founding, it has promoted technology education on a grand scale, reaching more than 1,000,000 students, parents, and educators.

Super Scratch Programming Adventure! is our second of three books about Scratch and the first to be translated into English. This book highlights the playful spirit of learning to program with Scratch, which inspires young people to apply digital technologies in imaginative and innovative ways.

We are very grateful to the MIT Media Lab, which has been our partner since LEAD was established in 2005. We are particularly appreciative of Professor Mitchel Resnick and Mr. Michael Smith-Welch, who have always been LEAD's staunchest supporters and greatest cheerleaders. Because of their unwavering belief in Scratch and in LEAD, you are now able to read this English edition.

We hope this book inspires you to design your very own games, projects, and more with Scratch.

Dr. Rosanna Wong Yick-ming, DBE, JP
Executive Director
The Hong Kong Federation of Youth Groups

A NOTE FOR PARENTS AND EDUCATORS

Scratch opens up an exciting world of computer programming for kids and other beginning programmers. To follow along with this book and use Scratch 3.0, you'll need:

- A computer with a recent Web browser (Chrome 63 or later, Edge 15 or later, Firefox 57 or later, or Safari 11 or later) with Adobe Flash Player version 10.2 or later installed
- A display that's 1024 × 768 or larger
- A reliable Internet connection
- A microphone and speakers (or headphones) to record and listen to music
- Although Scratch 3.0 runs on mobile devices, the projects in this book require a computer with a keyboard and mouse.

Open your browser and navigate to *http://scratch.mit.edu/*. You can create a new Scratch project without logging in by clicking the **Create** button. You'll want to eventually **Join Scratch** to create your own account and save your projects (see how in "Join the Community!" on page 15).

You should download the projects used in this book from *https://nostarch.com/superscratch3*. This online resource includes complete working projects, custom sprites, and a short *Getting Started with Scratch* guide produced by the Scratch team.

NOTE *The Resources file includes two versions of each game in the book. One version is a completely finished and playable game, perfect for young learners and anyone who wants to build on the games in the book. The second set of projects has no programming added, so that students can follow along with the programming instructions in this book. Remember, there's no wrong way to play with Scratch!*

BUT WHAT IS SCRATCH, ANYWAY?

Scratch is a graphical programming language that you can use for free. By simply dragging and dropping colored blocks, you can create interactive stories, games, animation, music, art, and presentations. You can even upload your creations to the Internet to share them with Scratch programmers from around the world. Scratch is designed for play, self-directed learning, and design.

WHERE DID THE NAME SCRATCH COME FROM?

Scratch is named for the way that hip-hop disc jockeys (DJs) creatively combine pieces of music, using a technique called *scratching*. In the same way, Scratch programmers join different media (images, photos, sound effects, and so on) in exciting ways to create something entirely new.

WHO CREATED SCRATCH?

Scratch is a project funded by the US National Science Foundation (NSF). It was developed by the Massachusetts Institute of Technology (MIT) Media Lab's Lifelong Kindergarten Group.

WHO IS SCRATCH FOR?

Scratch was developed for young people aged 8 and up to help them develop creative learning skills for the 21st century. When kids create programs, they learn important mathematical and computer concepts that improve their creative thinking, logical reasoning, problem solving, and collaboration skills.

This creative thinking spiral is from Professor Resnick's article, "Sowing the Seeds of a More Creative Society," published in *ISTE (International Society for Technology in Education)*.

Designing Scratch projects challenges kids to think creatively, and learning how to overcome obstacles and solve problems builds confidence. This gives learners an advantage later in life.

IS IT EASY TO USE SCRATCH?

Scratch was designed to prevent the common beginner pitfalls in traditional programming languages, like misspelling and errors in consistency. Instead of typing commands, programming in Scratch is performed by dragging and joining programming blocks. This graphical interface allows users to easily control the way in which different types of commands react to each other. Additionally, each block can fit with another only if it makes computational sense. Colorized categories help organize and group different sets of related commands based on their particular functions.

Since programs in Scratch run in real time, they can be edited and tested at any given moment, even while the program is running. This allows users to easily experiment with new ideas or to repeatedly test their improvements!

HOW MANY LANGUAGES DOES SCRATCH SUPPORT?

Scratch can be used in 50 different languages. Choose your language from the pull-down menu at the bottom of the Scratch website.

WHERE CAN YOU USE SCRATCH?

You can use Scratch at schools, libraries, community centers, and home. Even though Scratch is designed for young people aged 8 and up, younger children can also learn to design and create alongside their parents or siblings.

Scratch is used around the world in elementary, middle, and high schools. Computer science professors also use Scratch as a means of introducing programming concepts to college students.

HOW CAN SCRATCH BE USED TO EDUCATE IN SCHOOLS?

Schools can use Scratch to aid teachers in subjects like mathematics, English, music, art, design, and information technology. Scratch is designed for exploration and experimentation, so it supports many different learning styles.

No matter what they use Scratch for—creative storytelling, unique video games, or simple demonstrations of programming concepts—Scratch will provide a space for students to explore and imagine. By engaging in design-based activity individually or in groups, students will be motivated to learn.

Here are just a few of the things that students have used Scratch to do:

- A school in New York City used Scratch to build simulations of the spread of infectious diseases.
- A group of teenagers in India used Scratch to make an animated map of their village, illustrating environmental concerns where they live.

- Students at a university in Istanbul used Scratch to examine video game culture by rapidly prototyping their own games and testing the games with the public.
- English students in a middle school in California used Scratch to build a random story generator.
- Students in an elementary school in Russia used Scratch to build their own personalized tutorials for learning about the coordinate system and trigonometry.
- High school students in Michigan used Scratch to build a physics simulator.

The possibilities are endless. It is our sincere hope that this book inspires students to create their own games, stories, and more.

JOIN THE COMMUNITY!

Because Scratch is online, kids can easily share their own Scratch projects with their friends, family, and teachers. Once someone shares their work publicly on the Scratch website, other Scratch programmers can remix their projects, give them feedback, and more.

Follow these steps to join Scratch:

1. Visit the Scratch home page (*http://scratch.mit.edu/*) and click **Join Scratch** to register (you only need to register once).
2. Choose a username (don't use your real name), and then fill out the rest of the information. If the person registering is under 13, Scratch will ask for the email address of a parent or guardian.

NOTE *Once you share a project, everyone in the whole world can see what you've made! Make sure that your kids or students know to keep their personal information private.*

As long as they have the username and password at hand, kids can find games to play through the project gallery, remix them, and share their thoughts with others from around the world! To see how someone else's game was built, just click the **See Inside** button (See inside). To add to the program, click the big orange **Remix** button (Remix).

To share your own projects with the rest of the world, click the big **Share** button (Share) in the Scratch editor. To make a project private again, click the **Unshare** button in the **My Stuff** listing.

Just remember that as a member of the Scratch community, you'll be sharing projects and ideas with people of all ages, all levels of experience, and all parts of the world. So be sure to:

- Be respectful of other players
- Be constructive when commenting
- Help keep the site friendly and fun
- Keep personal information private

For more ideas and information about sharing and remixing projects, visit *http://wiki.scratch.mit.edu/wiki/Remix*.

MY COMPUTER CAN'T RUN SCRATCH 3.0!

If your computer doesn't meet the requirements listed on page 10, you can still download and install Scratch 2.0 (*https://scratch.mit.edu/download/scratch2*). Scratch 2.0 projects are compatible with the Web-based Scratch 3.0, and you can still share your projects on the Scratch website using Scratch 2.0. (Unfortunately, Scratch 2.0 cannot read programs created in the Scratch 3.0 software.)

You can download free PDF versions of Chapters 1 and 2, which explain how the older 2.0 interface works, by visiting *https://nostarch.com/superscratch3*. You can also find versions of the book's games that are compatible with 2.0 on that page.

I'M AN EDUCATOR USING SCRATCH

Awesome! This book is great place to start for classes and after-school programs. You'll want to download the free Educator's Guide at *https://nostarch.com/superscratch3*. Visit the official Scratch educator's forum at *http://scratched.media.mit.edu/* to exchange resources, share success stories, and ask questions of other educators already using Scratch as an educational tool.

I STILL HAVE OTHER QUESTIONS...

You can find more information on the Scratch website:

- Visit the Scratch FAQ at *http://info.scratch.mit.edu/Support/Scratch_FAQ/*.
- Visit the Scratch Help at *http://scratch.mit.edu/help/*.

"Online Resources" on page 156 has other helpful links. For updates to this book, visit *https://nostarch.com/superscratch3*.

MEET THE CAST

Mitch
A computer science student who loves to make cool programs, he's passionate about movies and art, too! Mitch is an all-around good guy.

The Cosmic Defenders: Gobo, Fabu, and Pele
The Cosmic Defenders are trans-dimensional space aliens who can travel through space and time. Formally deputized by the Galactic Council, the Cosmic Defender's duty is to maintain the balance of the universe.

The Dark Wizard
He is a shapeless yet powerful and vengeful spirit, whose origins are unknown. Nothing can stop his ambition of destroying the order of space and time.

The Dark Minions
These pesky foes are Cosmic Defenders who have fallen to the dark side. They work for the Dark Wizard now.

Scratchy
An energetic cat living in cyber-space, Scratchy is exactly what you'd expect from a cat on the Internet. He's quite curious and impulsive.

RIDING A FLARE FROM THE SUN

1 STAGE

STAGE 1

BREAKING THE SPELL!

➕ Chapter Focus

Let's get to know Scratch! We'll also learn about *sprites* and *coordinates*.

✏️ The Game

We need to get Scratchy the cat moving again. We'll make him dance across the Stage.

Blocks Palette

To follow along with the Secret Manual, you first need to open Scratch. Once you **Create** a new project, you'll see Scratchy the cat on a white backdrop. The cat doesn't do anything yet because he doesn't have any programs. Scratch calls Scratchy the cat—and all the other characters and objects we add to a project—a *sprite*. Soon, we'll start giving him directions to move by dragging the blue blocks into the middle of the screen.

The command blocks you can give a sprite are here. We'll stack these commands together to break the magic spell and get Scratchy back on his feet. The blocks here are all blue, as they're from the **Motion** palette.

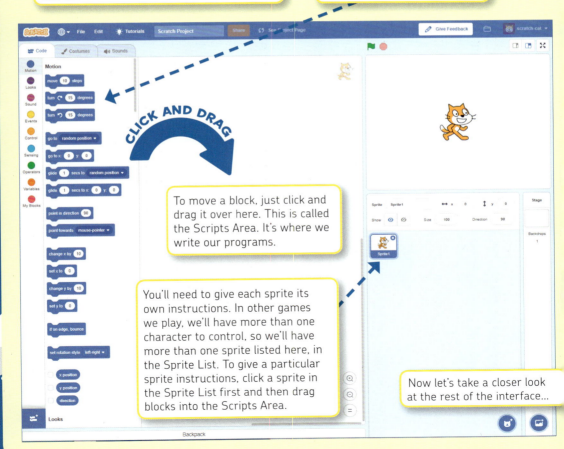

CLICK AND DRAG

To move a block, just click and drag it over here. This is called the Scripts Area. It's where we write our programs.

You'll need to give each sprite its own instructions. In other games we play, we'll have more than one character to control, so we'll have more than one sprite listed here, in the Sprite List. To give a particular sprite instructions, click a sprite in the Sprite List first and then drag blocks into the Scripts Area.

Now let's take a closer look at the rest of the interface...

A Guided Tour of the Scratch Interface!

Blocks Palette
Each of these nine buttons lets you choose different types of blocks for programming your sprites. You can combine these command blocks in stacks to create programs that control objects on the screen.

The green flag starts the game and the red flag stops the game.

Play the game full screen.

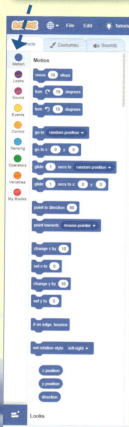

Give your project a new name.

Coding Area
Here's where you build your programs. Stacking blocks together here lets you control the sprites in your project. Click one of the three tabs at the top to change to other functions:

Code: Allows you to drag command blocks from the Palette and put them together to write a program

Costumes: Allows you to draw, import, or edit images for a sprite

Sounds: Allows you to record or import sound files for a sprite to use

Stage
Displays your creation

Sprite List
Here are the characters and objects you've created, including the Stage itself. Click the icons to edit each sprite individually.

Sprite Info
Contains the Sprite name, Position, Direction, Size, and Hide/Show tools

Adding a New Sprite
Select one of the following four buttons to add a sprite:
- **Choose a Sprite:** pick a sprite from Scratch's built-in library
- **Paint:** draw your own sprite
- **Surprise:** let Scratch choose a random one
- **Upload Sprite:** use an image you already have

23

STAGE 1

Sprite Information
You might have noticed a blue **highlight** around Scratchy when you select his sprite in the Sprite List. Try clicking on a sprite to see the sprite's name, position, size, and direction (angle) it is facing.

This is how you can rename the Scratchy sprite. Right now it's *Sprite1*. Don't you think that's a little boring? Try renaming this sprite.

CLICK HERE

Rotation Settings
Try clicking in the space marked Direction, and move the arrow that appears—see what happens to Scratchy's orientation. Click the two small arrows underneath the circle, then compare what happens when you move the large arrow.

Now, onto the fun stuff. To use Scratch to program movements, you first have to understand how Scratch positions things.

Click the Backdrops icon in the bottom right of the screen, and select **Choose a Backdrop**.

Note: Sprites have *costumes* while the Stage has *backdrops*.

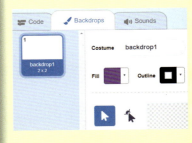

Choose the *xy-grid* backdrop and click **OK** to use it.

Now you can see exactly how Scratch positions objects. Everything is on a grid with two axes:

y-axis: A vertical line that marks up and down positions; ranges from −180 (lowest) to +180 (highest)

x-axis: A horizontal line that marks left and right positions; ranges from −240 (farthest left) to +240 (farthest right)

Scratchy's default position is at the point where the x-axis and y-axis meet. His coordinates are (X: 0, Y: 0).

Now we can program movements for Scratchy the cat! But first, try dragging him to the top of the Stage, as shown on the right.

You'll notice that the current coordinates of a sprite are shown in the Sprite bar, below the Stage.

To make sure we're giving Scratchy the cat instructions, click him in the Sprite List (the box at the bottom left of the screen). Switch to the **Code** tab in the Coding Area and then click the **Motion** palette button. Click and drag out the command block `go to x:0 y:0` to the Coding Area. Although you can scroll up and down through all command blocks, the palette buttons are a neat shortcut.

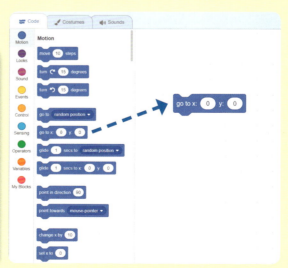

STAGE 1

Click the number of a coordinate to change it. Set x to 0 and set y to 125. Now click the block to run it! Scratchy goes right to that position. We've just written our first program! It's really that simple.

We want Scratchy to move around, but at the moment, he moves too fast for us to see! To make him move more slowly, click the **Control** palette and drag out the command `wait 1 secs` to the Coding Area. Make sure to drag it under your blue command block. Wait for a gray box to appear and then release the mouse.

The two commands are joined together! Now change the time to 0.1 secs.

Tip: If you want to separate the commands, simply drag away the block. If you want to delete a block, simply drag it back to the palette. Give it a try. To move a big stack of blocks, click and drag the topmost block in the stack.

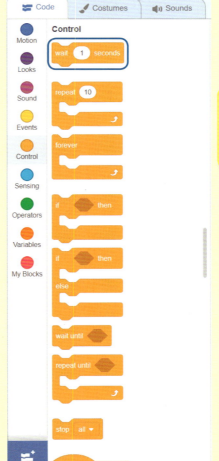

Next, right-click the top of the two blocks and select **Duplicate** to make five copies.

Type these coordinates in your own program, so it matches this picture. When you're finished, click the whole command block to make Scratchy jump around in a pentagon shape!

```
go to x: 0 y: 125
wait 0.1 seconds
go to x: 150 y: 30
wait 0.1 seconds
go to x: 100 y: -120
wait 0.1 seconds
go to x: -100 y: -120
wait 0.1 seconds
go to x: -150 y: 30
wait 0.1 seconds
```

```
forever
  go to x: 0 y: 125
  wait 0.1 seconds
  go to x: 150 y: 30
  wait 0.1 seconds
  go to x: 100 y: -120
  wait 0.1 seconds
  go to x: -100 y: -120
  wait 0.1 seconds
  go to x: -150 y: 30
  wait 0.1 seconds
```

To make him move in a loop continuously, drag out the command block `forever` from the **Control** palette and place it at the top of the code. Click the block, and it will actually run! Click to stop Scratchy from moving around. You can test any program in this way—just click it with your mouse.

Tip: Whenever you're writing scripts, you'll want to test them every now and then to see if they work the way you expect.

Now let's make Scratchy glide around instead of jumping from point to point. To do this, click the **Motion** palette, drag out five `glide` commands, and join them together. Follow the picture on the right, and copy the seconds and coordinates. Once you're finished, click the script to see the results!

```
glide 0.1 secs to x: 150 y: 30
glide 0.1 secs to x: -100 y: -120
glide 0.1 secs to x: 0 y: 125
glide 0.1 secs to x: 100 y: -120
glide 0.1 secs to x: -150 y: 30
```

```
when clicked
forever
  go to x: 0 y: 125
  wait 0.1 seconds
  go to x: 150 y: 30
  wait 0.1 seconds
  go to x: 100 y: -120
  wait 0.1 seconds
  go to x: -100 y: -120
  wait 0.1 seconds
  go to x: -150 y: 30
  wait 0.1 seconds
  glide 0.1 secs to x: 150 y: 30
  glide 0.1 secs to x: -100 y: -120
  glide 0.1 secs to x: 0 y: 125
  glide 0.1 secs to x: 100 y: -120
  glide 0.1 secs to x: -150 y: 30
```

Now we can join these two programs together! From the **Events** palette, drag out the `When clicked` command and put it at the top of your two scripts.

Tip: We'll often need multiple scripts to start at the same time, and using the `When clicked` command will help us do that.

STAGE 1

Because we used the `When ⚑ clicked` command, we can use these buttons above the Stage to start (⚑) and stop (🔴) the game.

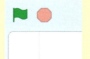

Click the Add Extension icon in the bottom left corner of the screen, to add the Pen extension.

Pen
Draw with your sprites.

Next, click the **Pen** palette and drag out the four green Pen blocks shown on the right. Now when Scratchy moves, he'll draw a *magic star web*!

UH-OH! THERE'S A BUG!

Occasionally, when you run your program, there is a *software bug*. This is the most exciting part of computer programming: discovering an error in something you have made and then solving the problem. In this case, sometimes Scratchy will draw an odd line at the beginning of the program.

If we drag Scratchy anywhere else on the Stage and then press ⚑, he draws an extra line because he starts in the wrong place. Try doing this multiple times to see if you can spot the bug.

28

This software bug can be fixed by adding some more code—that is, new blocks—to your program. In this case, simply place a new `go to` block (from the blue **Motion** palette) above the green Pen blocks and below the `When clicked` block.

With this little correction, Scratchy will always begin drawing from the correct position in the grid. The bug is gone!

Let's add a whole new program to make a magic star web that changes colors. Build a second stack of blocks that uses the `change pen color by` command and see what happens.

Isn't that cool? You can give a single sprite more than one set of blocks! Scratchy now has two programs. This tiny second program sure makes a big difference in how the game looks.

29

STAGE 1

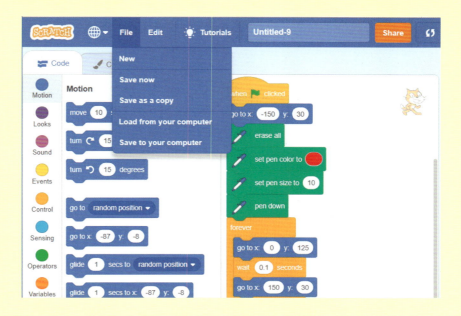

Remember to save this file so you can play with it later!

If you are logged into Scratch, the website stores all of your projects into **My Stuff** so you can easily find them. The website saves your progress every so often, but you can save manually too: **File ▸ Save Now**. You can also save different versions of your programs to make sure you don't lose older versions of your games and can safely experiment—**File ▸ Save as a Copy** creates a new version of your project in My Stuff. If you want to download a version for yourself, try **File ▸ Save to your computer**. Then save it in a safe spot!

Scratchy's Challenge!!

Can you edit this program to make Scratchy draw different kinds of shapes? Give it a try!

ENTERING SPACE

STAGE 2

STAGE 2

2 STAGE

A SPACE ODYSSEY!

➕ Chapter Focus

Learn to design new costumes and program a sprite's movements, reactions, and sound effects.

✏️ The Game

Avoid the lightning bolts and collect seven dimensional strings. Once you've got them all, the Monolith will appear!

To make things really easy, let's start by opening a blank project called **02 - A Space Odyssey.sb2**. This project has all the sprites you'll need, but none of the programming yet. To open a file, click **File ▸ Upload from your computer**.

But let's try making some sprites of our own, so you can make changes to this game's characters and invent your own games, too! Click Scratchy's sprite icon in the Sprite List, and then click the **Costumes** tab. You'll see the Paint Editor—just be sure to click the costume you want to change.

At the top of the Paint Editor, you can give your Costume a name. We can then reference the costume names in our programming.

If your Paint Editor looks different, it could be because you haven't opened the blank project file (*02 - A Space Odyssey .sb2*) that has Scratchy's astronaut costume.

Scratch has two modes for editing graphics—on the right is **Bitmap** mode. See page 38 to learn more about editing in Vector mode.

Here's where all the tools are. The **Brush** and **Eraser** tools make it easy to draw.

Use the **Fill** tool to color big parts of your drawing at once. You can set a single color from the palette sliders, or use a gradient effect from the Tool Options.

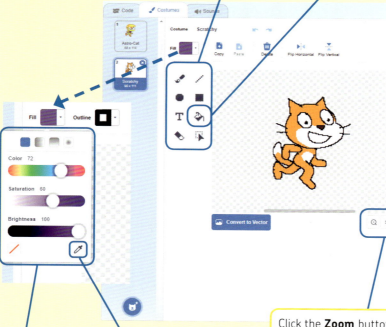

The **Eyedropper** tool will match the current color to any color you click in your image.

Click the **Zoom** buttons (the magnifying glasses on the bottom right) to zoom in or out on your creations. This will make it easier to draw! Clicking the equals sign (**=**) shows you exactly how your sprite will appear on the Stage.

If you're not sure what a button does, simply hover your cursor over it, and a description will appear!

Tool Options

Whatever tool you are using, the options for the tool will appear at the bottom of the Paint Editor. For example, the size of the Brush or Eraser can be adjusted if you want to make a big drawing or add fine detail. Just click and enter a number or use the arrows to set the right size.

You pick a color for your tool here, too.

You also have tools to draw rectangles and ellipses. Can you give Scratchy a stovepipe hat like Abe Lincoln using the **Rectangle** and **Ellipse** tools?

These shapes can be empty inside or filled in. Try experimenting with different colors for the inside and outside. If you press the SHIFT key when you start to draw, you'll have a perfect circle or square! (You can also use this SHIFT trick when using the **Line** tool to draw a straight line.) Try rotating your shapes using the handle on the top of the box.

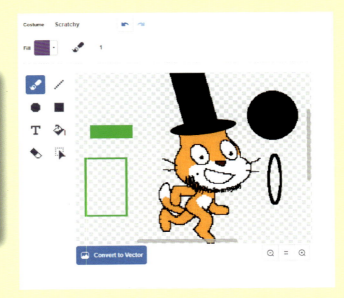

The **Text** tool lets you add writing to your sprite. We'll use this tool when we need to give the player instructions for our games. If you want to move the text, simply click and drag the black box that surrounds your text.

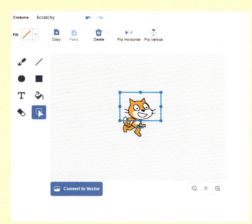

To use the **Select** tool, use your mouse to create a frame around a certain area. Then you can do all sorts of things to the selected part of your costume:

- Click and drag the selection to move it to a new location.
- Resize, smush, or stretch the image using the handles on the sides of the box.
- Rotate the selection by clicking and dragging the handle at the top center of the box.
- Press and hold the CTRL key and C key at the same time to copy the image area (Mac users can use ⌘-C instead). Then press CTRL-V (⌘-V on a Mac) to paste your selection, as many times as you like.
- Press the DELETE key to erase the selection or ESC to remove the frame without changing anything.

STAGE 2

Vector Mode

You may have noticed that when you edit other sprites in Scratch, you don't see the same Paint Editor tools. Some newer sprites are *vector* art—that's just a fancy way to say they're made of shapes, instead of pixels. Vector art have small filesizes, but they are great quality—and they can be resized without losing quality.

Note: For simplicity's sake, all of the graphics in this book use Bitmap mode. But your custom projects can use a mix of vector and bitmap graphics.

You can switch from Scratch's **Bitmap** mode (the one seen earlier) to **Vector** mode by clicking the **Convert to Vector** button at the bottom left of the Paint Editor. The difference between using these two tools in Scratch is like the difference between Adobe Photoshop and Illustrator—or GIMP and Inkscape. Use whichever Paint Editor mode you like the most!

You can import SVG files into Scratch's vector editor. In Vector mode, you can squeeze and shape lines, reshape, and ungroup. Here's how the Vector mode works.

Try opening a vector graphic from Scratch's library, and give editing one a try.

The Backpack

Here's a cool feature. If you're logged into the Scratch website, you'll see something called the **Backpack** at the very bottom of the screen. Click it, and it'll open up. Yours will be empty until you throw some sprites in it.

Your Backpack lets you share sprites and scripts between projects. If you play a really cool game on the Scratch website and want to use the character in an entirely new project, just click and drag the sprite right into your Backpack.

When you create a new project of your own, just open the Backpack again and drag the sprite out. You can write all new programs, or use the ones that were already with the sprite. You can even use your Backpack to store programs you want to reuse!

STAGE 2

Once you know how to use the Paint Editor's tools, Scratchy can put on his space suit! Go ahead and draw your own, or use the costume that's already in the project.

Now we have the main character for our game: Scratchy the astronaut!

Next, let's take a look at the other sprites in the game. You can use the art that's already in the game, or draw new artwork yourself! Click 🖌 to draw a new sprite.

First, take a look at the String and the Monolith. They are two costumes for the same sprite, **String**. If they were two separate sprites, we'd have to write two programs. But now we can make this sprite switch costumes and write only one program.

Now for our third new sprite, some scary **Lightning**! The player will need to avoid the lighting.

We also need some instructions to appear at the start of the game. We'll call this sprite **Banner**.

Get 7 Dimension Strings
to open the Stargate!!

Avoid the Lightning
or you will disappear!!

2 STAGE

Next, let's look at the Stage. I used artwork of a black hole from NASA! You can draw a new backdrop if you like. Click the Stage on the right of the Sprite List, and then click the **Backdrops** tab at the top left of the screen.

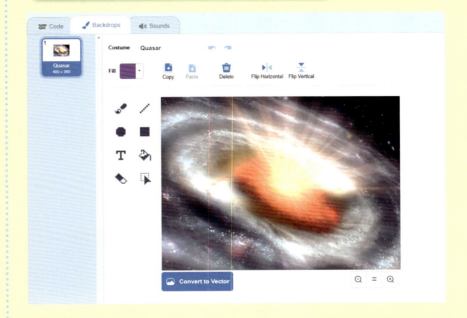

Now that we have a bunch of sprites for the game, you can see how everything appears in the Sprite List. To give a sprite new instructions or costumes, you'll first have to click it in the Sprite List. Let's start by giving Scratchy the astronaut his programming.

Let's write our first program ❶ for Scratchy! Make sure he's selected in the Sprite List and you've clicked the **Scripts** tab. His first program is a short one that makes him bounce up and down a little. This makes him look like he's floating in zero gravity!

❶

❷ For program ❷, we'll make a *conditional*—if something is true, then something else will happen. In the **Control** palette, drag out an `if` block. Then for the diamond shape, drag the **Sensing** block `key _____ pressed?`. Right below the `if`, put what you want to happen when the statement is true. Drag out the rest of these commands to form the complete program. Now you can move Scratchy up, down, left, and right by using the keyboard!

Now we'll give Scratchy two more programs. We'll need to program them individually, and then use `When ⚑ clicked` to make them all run at the same time.

❸

❹

Let's write programs ❸ and ❹. Click the **Control** and **Looks** palettes and drag out these commands.

Program ❸ controls which costume Scratchy wears, and program ❹ makes Scratchy become invisible like a ghost each time he gets struck by lightning.

When you've finished all of this, Scratchy's programming is complete!

Next, let's click the **Banner** sprite. We just need a simple program to make these instructions appear at the start of the game. The `repeat 2` loop using the `show` and `hide` blocks makes our instructions flash, so the game is even more exciting.

43

2 STAGE

Now we can add sound effects to the game! I've already added a few, but you can change things up. First, click the **Stage** in the Sprite List. Then click its **Sounds** tab. You can create whatever kind of sound effects or music you like for your Scratch projects. You can even record your own sounds right in the Scratch program.

If you click the **Record** button, a sound recorder will pop up. You can click the round button to record speech or sound effects through a microphone. If this is the first time you've recorded sound, your browser may ask for permission to use your microphone—if this happens, click OK to allow just the Scratch website to have access. You'll notice that Scratch marks the silent sections to be cut out. You can adjust these. When you're finished, click **Save**.

Note: To record your own sounds, you'll need a microphone attached to the computer. To listen to sound effects and music, you'll need speakers.

If you want to use sounds that are prerecorded, you can press 🔊 to use Scratch's sound library, or 📁 to choose files from your own computer (MP3 and compressed WAV, AIF, and AU formats are supported).

Now we can add some simple programs to the Stage. Program ❶ makes its backdrop change colors. In program ❷, use the **Sound** palette to add a song to the Stage.

❶
```
when 🚩 clicked
switch backdrop to Quasar
forever
    change color effect by 25
    wait 0.1 seconds
```

❷
```
when 🚩 clicked
forever
    set volume to 100 %
    play sound Techno1 until done
```

Next, we can add some sound effects to the String and Lightning sprites to make the game more exciting! Test how you like my sound effects, and make your own if you like.

You can record a sound yourself and then change it using the **Effects** menu. Try reversing what you record to make it sound really weird!

Click the **Lightning** sprite, and write a program so that whenever Scratchy touches a lightning bolt, a sound will play.

```
when 🚩 clicked
wait 1 seconds
forever
    if <touching Astro-Cat?> then
        set volume to 30 %
        play sound Thunder until done
```

STAGE 2

The **Lightning** sprite needs some more programs. Go to the **Control**, **Events**, **Looks**, and **Operators** palettes and program these commands to have the lightning bolt randomly grow bigger or smaller, making the game more magical.

Next, write this program to make the lightning disappear whenever Scratchy touches it and to control the way it moves.

The lightning's vertical position (y-axis) changes because we repeat eight times the subtraction of 40 steps (-40) from its original y-coordinate of 260. To make the lightning move differently, you can change and play with these numbers.

So that the lightning bolt makes Scratchy disappear, we must make sure that each time it moves—that is, the position of its y-axis changes—the program will check if it touches Scratchy.

Tip: Sometimes when you've used the `hide` and `show` blocks, a sprite can disappear while you're working on the program—running it, testing it, and checking for bugs. Simply click the `show` block in the **Looks** palette to make the sprite appear again. (You can also check the **show** box in the Sprite Information pane.)

Now it's time to program the **String** sprite. Make sure you click it in the Sprite List first! Program ❶ makes it change color, just like our Stage. Program ❷ will give it a simple animation, using the fisheye effect.

Now for a big program. Let's start by dragging out the blocks you can see in ❸. These will control how the String costume spins and moves.

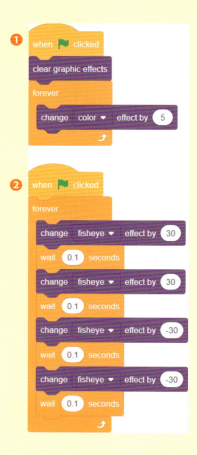

Then add to your program so that it looks like ❹. This will make your dimensional string appear in a random place on the Stage seven different times. The `say` blocks and `play sound` blocks at the end of the program make sure the player knows Scratchy has grabbed a dimensional string.

❹

```
repeat 7
  go to x: pick random 210 to -210 y: pick random 150 to -150
  show
  repeat until touching Astro-Cat ?
    change y by 1
    turn ↻ 5 degrees
    wait 0.1 seconds
    change y by -1
    turn ↻ 5 degrees
    wait 0.1 seconds
  say Got it!
  set volume to 30 %
  start sound Humming
  wait 0.2 seconds
  say
  hide
  wait 0.3 seconds
```

We're not done yet! This is a big script.

❺ Add a `When ⚑ clicked` block at the top of our script and some instructions at the very bottom so that once Scratchy has collected seven dimensional strings, the String sprite will change to its Monolith costume. When that happens, the player wins the game. Make sure your finished program looks like ❺.

Now you're done! Nice work!

STAGE 2

After saving the file, you can enjoy your final creation! Make the Stage full screen and click 🏁 to begin a new round.

Scratchy's Challenge!!

Add more lightning bolts to give yourself a challenge. Or you could replace the lightning bolt with a big, scary space monster you drew yourself! Give it a try!

TRAPPED BY MONA LISA'S SMILE

STAGE 3

STAGE 3

THE LOUVRE

STAGE 3

➕ Chapter Focus

Let's learn how to control the *flow* of a game. You'll see how to keep score using *variables* and control the order of the game using *broadcasts*.

🖉 The Game

This game is actually two games in one. First, you'll face Rata's quiz. Then you'll have to put the *Mona Lisa* back together in a puzzle game. If you get the answer wrong three times, the game ends and you lose!

This program has some tricky custom graphics. So let's start out by opening a blank file called **03 – Louvre Puzzle.sb2** (File ▸ Upload from your computer), which has these sprites in it. Take a look around. You can see that the Stage has a backdrop that shows the Louvre. We just don't have any programs yet!

Then we'll add a program that makes the Stage play music. The `forever` block is a special kind of command we call a *loop*. Any sound effect or music you add here keeps playing again and again, so make sure you like how it sounds!

Photo Credit: Raphael Frey

STAGE 3

Now click the sprite for **Rata**, in the Sprite List. Make sure you like how he looks. Since we selected him, now we can give him some programs!

❶ Write program ❶ first. This `forever` loop makes Rata float up and down.

For program ❷, go to the **Looks**, **Sensing**, and **Operators** palettes, and use the `ask` and `say` blocks. This program asks the first question of Rata's quiz. We've made it a multiple-choice question, so the answer must be A or B.

If you noticed back in program ❷, there's a command that says `broadcast question2` if you get the right answer. *Broadcasts* are like big announcements to all the programs in your project. They're a great way to connect related parts of a game. So let's try writing two more questions as new programs ❸ and ❹. These two programs wait for broadcasts `question2` and `question3` to start using the `when I receive` block.

❸
```
when I receive question2
forever
    ask Where was it painted? (A) Madrid, Spain (B) Florence, Italy and wait
    if answer = A then
        say Try again! for 1 seconds
    if answer = B then
        say You are right! for 1 seconds
        broadcast question3
        stop this script
```

❹
```
when I receive question3
forever
    ask Where is it now? (A) The Louvre, Paris (B) The Colosseum, Rome and wait
    if answer = A then
        say You are right! for 1 seconds
        say Now try to solve this puzzle! for 2 seconds
        hide
        broadcast puzzle
        stop this script
    if answer = B then
        say Try again! for 1 seconds
```

When the player answers all three questions correctly, the `puzzle` broadcast signal in program ❹ tells the game that the quiz is over and the puzzle half of our game should now begin.

STAGE 3

Now take a look at the **Puzzle** sprite. This isn't just a single image—it's a sprite with a bunch of costumes. The sprite's costumes include instructions for the player, as well as the puzzle itself!

The final two costumes display the winning screen and the message that appears when you lose.

Let's take a closer look. First, we'll display the costume that shows instructions for the player.

Memorize the picture sequence!

Then we'll display the four parts of the *Mona Lisa*. These costumes display the sequence that players have to remember to win!

The next three costumes display more game instructions and a start screen.

Repeat the sequence correctly!

Start Now!!

Finally, we have two costumes for the winning and losing screens.

STAGE 3

For this big sprite, we'll need a lot of programs. Let's start by adding a special kind of command called a *variable*. Variables are good for keeping track of numbers that change during a game, like scores, player health, player lives, and more.

Click **Make a Variable** in the **Data** palette, and call it Chance. The new Chance variable is how the computer knows how many times the player gets another chance to solve the puzzle before losing.

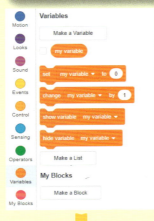

Now for the programs themselves. Add scripts ❶ and ❷. Script ❶ just hides our variable Chance during the quiz part of the game. Next, script ❷ determines how the Puzzle sprite should change costumes—just as described on pages 56–57. After it's done switching costumes, it broadcasts start.

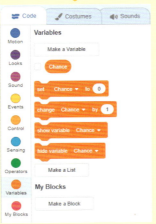

Then we'll add four different scripts: one for each right answer to the puzzle. If the player presses the wrong arrow, the sprite changes its costume and a broadcast called wrong is broadcast. We'll use this broadcast to control the Chance variable.

Tip: You can use the Duplicate tool (⬇) in the Sprite Toolbar to save some time dragging out blocks.

Notice how the broadcast named 1 at the end of script ❸ starts script ❹. Likewise, script ❺ starts only when I receive 3, which is broadcast by script ❹ when the player presses the correct arrow. With all of the correct arrows pressed in script ❻, we signal a new broadcast called win.

STAGE 3

❼ when I receive wrong
change Chance by -1
wait 1 seconds

❽ when 🏁 clicked
set Chance to 3
forever
 if Chance < 1 then
  switch costume to monalisa_lose
  stop all

❾ when I receive win
switch costume to monalisa_win
stop all

Finally, add three more programs to the Puzzle. Program ❼ subtracts 1 from the *Chance* variable any time it receives the *wrong* broadcast. Programs ❽ and ❾ control when the winning and losing screens appear.

That's it! Remember to save your project, and then give the game a try. Let's see if you can win this!

Scratchy's Challenge!!

Can you use the `ask` block and broadcasts to create a personality test? How about a flash-card game to learn words in a new language? Give it a try!

DEFEND HONG KONG'S TECHNOCORE

STAGE 4

HACK ATTACK

STAGE 4

➕ Chapter Focus
Learn to control sprites with the mouse, program objects to bounce back, and start a game by pressing the spacebar.

✏️ The Game
Help Scratchy attack flying viruses and stop them from touching the server at the bottom of the screen. If you successfully block 30 viruses, you win the game!

Let's start by opening the blank project **04 – Hack Attack!.sb2** (File ▶ Upload from your computer). I used a sparkly photo of Hong Kong's skyline as my Stage. You can use whatever you like!

Did you know you can add programs to the Stage, too? We can add this program to make our city glow!

STAGE 4

Now let's take a look at the **Instructions** sprite. It tells the player how the game works. We'll write two programs to control it.

```
Protect Hong Kong!
Defend the server from virus attacks

Click your mouse to move Scratchy!
Press <SPACE> to start!
```

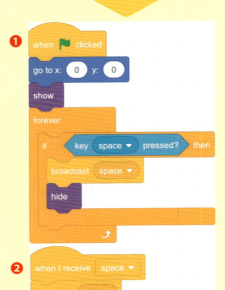

Program ❶ makes the sprite show up at the start of the game and disappear when the player presses `space`, the spacebar on their keyboard.

Program ❷ makes the Instructions sprite broadcast `start` when it receives the `space` broadcast from program ❶. This will start the game!

Next, let's write some programs for Scratchy. Notice that he has two costumes already: one where he's just standing and another where he's jumping.

So let's add some programs to control how Scratchy looks. In program ❶, we `hide` him before the `start` broadcast is received. In program ❷, we control how Scratchy switches costumes. Whenever the player's mouse is clicked—that is, whenever `mouse down?`—Scratchy looks like he's jumping.

65

STAGE 4

❸

But how does the player control Scratchy? Program ❸ lets you control Scratchy with the mouse, showing him only when the `start` broadcast is received.

Program ❹ makes a speech bubble saying "OH NO!!" appear whenever the Scratchy sprite receives the `Oh` signal. We'll broadcast `Oh` whenever a virus manages to hit the server.

Tip: By using the mouse instead of the keyboard, the player has a lot of control over Scratchy, who will move very quickly for this game. But remember—every game is different! Sometimes the keyboard works well, too.

Time to program a new sprite! Switch to the **Server**. It should look like the image below, but we want it centered and at the bottom of the screen. Add this simple program so that the Server appears in the correct place.

Next, we'll program our computer opponent! The sprite called **Virus** has a set of costumes of letters spelling V-I-R-U-S.

Program ❶ hides the Virus until the game starts. Program ❷ makes the Virus switch costumes as it flies around.

Program ❸ for the Virus makes it fly around. It bounces whenever it bumps into Scratchy or the edges of the screen.

STAGE 4

Now we'll add more programs to the Virus to keep score. These programs use blocks from the **Control**, **Events**, and **Data** palettes to record and signal the conditions for winning and losing.

Program ❹ creates a new variable called score and the conditions we need to meet for the script to broadcast win. Your score will now appear on the Stage.

Program ❺ creates a variable called chance, which keeps track of how many times the Virus is allowed to touch the Server sprite before the player loses. We'll give Scratchy five chances to start. When you're out of chances, the program broadcasts lose. Just like the player's score, the number of tries the player has left is displayed on the Stage as chance.

Tip: When setting the rules for winning and losing in your games, use the greater-than symbol (>) or the less-than symbol (<) instead of the equal sign (=), as we do in programs ❹ and ❺. This will prevent the game from breaking when a variable changes too quickly!

Why might the variable change too fast in this game? Scratchy might touch the Virus a few times in quick succession, and the program won't realize that you've won the game.

Now let's look at the sprite for the winning screen. Programs ❶ and ❷ keep it hidden. Then program ❸ makes it appear when the `win` broadcast is received from the Virus sprite.

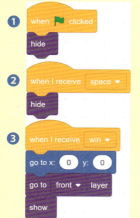

> You Win!!
> The city server is safe now!

The losing screen is pretty similar to the winning screen. To save time, we can select the **Duplicate** tool and click the winning screen to copy both the image and the programming!

All we need to do now is change the costume and the last program a bit.

> You Lose!!
> Press <SPACE> to try again!

STAGE 4

We're finished! After you save the file, hurry and help Scratchy the hacker defend the network from the virus attack!

Scratchy's Challenge!!

How would you make this game harder for the player? How about adding different kinds of viruses? What about turning this game into a two-player Ping-Pong match? Give it a try!

PENALTY KICK IN IPANEMA

STAGE 5

STAGE 5

RIO SHOOT-OUT

STAGE 5

➕ Chapter Focus
Learn how to program a soccer game with a targeting system, several related rules, interactive sound effects, and a vivid, animated backdrop!

✏️ The Game
Shoot penalty kicks and avoid the moving goalie. You'll win the game if you manage to score five out of eight tries!

Bull's-eye

Here's a look at the final game. We'll need to create a targeting system that will move over the goal. When you press the spacebar, you'll kick the ball where the bull's-eye is. But watch out—the goalkeeper will dive every time you kick the ball!

To start, you can upload the file **05 – Rio Shootout.sb2** (File ▸ Upload from your computer), which has all our sprites but no programming blocks yet.

You can draw your very own backdrop if you like!

I created a sprite for the clouds. Click the **Cloud** sprite, and then add a program to make it float up and down. This will make the backdrop livelier!

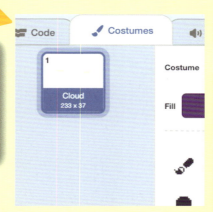

If there's a beach, there must be some waves! The **Wave** sprite is separate from the background, and we'll give it some programs of its own.

Since waves move up and down as well, their programming will be similar to the script for the clouds. Here's a little trick: First, select your Cloud sprite from the Sprite List, and drag its program to the picture icon of the Wave sprite in the Sprite List. Make sure your cursor is right over the Wave in the Sprite List, and then release your mouse. Now you've copied the programming for the Cloud sprite to the Wave sprite!

We can also change the Wave's script to make it move faster and more frequently than our clouds.

Then we can switch to our **Goalpost** sprite and write a program to set its position in the center of the field.

The goal's **Net** has its own sprite. Click it in the Sprite List, and then create this short program to set its position.

Now is a good time to test your program to make sure everything appears where you want it to. Try clicking ⚑. If your clouds float, the waves lap against the beach, and your goal and net are in the right place, let's move on to programming the game itself.

Next we'll program the **Bullseye** sprite, which shows where Mitch will kick the ball.

Program ❶ will make the bull's-eye zigzag across the goal.

For program ❷, add these two `set` commands from the **Data** palette in a `forever` loop. We'll use these variables to determine where the ball goes after Mitch kicks it. You'll need to create X and Y in the **Data** palette.

Tip: Since our player doesn't need this information, we can hide the variables from being displayed on the screen by deselecting them in the **Data** palette.

Then add in programs ❸ and ❹ to the Bullseye sprite. Program ❸ makes the bull's-eye continuously change color. Program ❹ makes the bull's-eye disappear when it receives the `shoot` broadcast. Now when Mitch kicks the ball, the bull's-eye will disappear.

STAGE 5

To make this game even more fun, we gave Pele the Keeper two costumes. That means we can program a simple animation by switching costumes.

We'll write two programs for Pele. Program ❶ sets his size, costume, and starting position and then animates him using the `next costume` command in a `forever` loop.

When he receives the shoot broadcast in program ❷, he'll "dive" to a random spot in the goal to try to stop the ball! The `pick random` blocks are in the **Operators** palette—just drag two right into the `glide` block.

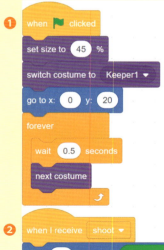

Now we'll move on to program the game's most important feature—the ball.

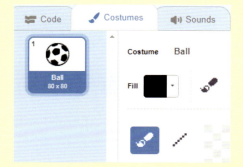

First, click the **Ball** in the Sprite List. Check out all the different sound effects I've added in the **Sounds** tab. You can also use your own custom sounds!

Next, write program ❶ to set its starting position and size, and then play the `Whistle` sound.

Tip: The first two blocks (`go to front layer` and `go back 1 layers`) adjust the layer value so the Ball will appear in front of the Net, Stage, and other sprites in the game.

❶

STAGE 5

By creating variables for `Ball` and `Score`, you can keep track of how many times the player has kicked the ball and how many times he has scored a point. Program ❷ sets the starting values for these variables.

Program ❸ will broadcast `shoot` whenever the spacebar is pressed. Notice how there's an `if` loop that uses a `not` block from the **Operators** palette to make sure the player isn't out of balls (`Ball > 0`) and hasn't won the game (`Score = 5`).

Program ❹ is a neat animation trick. It makes the ball shrink into the distance by using a negative value (`-2`) in the `change size by` block.

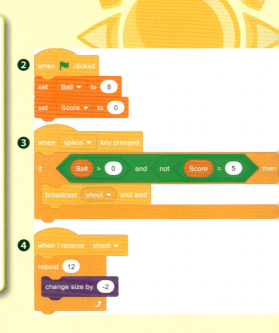

Program ❺ is quite special. First, it makes the ball `glide to` our variables `X` and `Y`. (Just drag them from the **Data** palette right into the `glide` block.) The two `if` loops contain the game's program for scoring. It broadcasts either `goal` or `miss`, depending on whether or not the ball touches Pele.

❺
```
when I receive  shoot
change  Ball  by  -1
glide  0.5  secs to x:  X   y:  Y
if  < touching Net ? > and < not < touching Keeper ? > >  then
    broadcast  goal  and wait

if  < touching Net ? > and < touching Keeper ? >  then
    broadcast  miss  and wait
```

80

You'll score a goal if you manage to sneak the ball by our goalkeeper Pele!

Now let's add some more programs to the Ball. In programs ❻ and ❼, we'll determine what happens after a goal or miss. Program ❻ will change the score by 1, while program ❼ will change it by 0. Whether the player scores or not, the ball returns to its original position after 1 second.

Programs ❽, ❾, and ❿ play sound effects for fun.

Next, we set the rules for winning and losing the game. Program ⓫ will broadcast won when the Score variable reaches 5. Programs ⓬ and ⓭ will broadcast lost after all the player's chances are up; that is, when Ball = 0. (Without program ⓭, the player can still lose even if he scores with his last ball.)

82

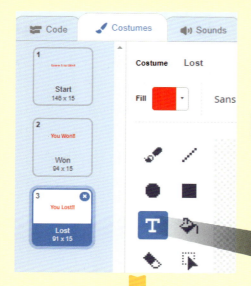

Finally, it's time to program our **Banner** sprite. It has three costumes for the game instructions (Start), the winning screen (Won), and the losing screen (Lost).

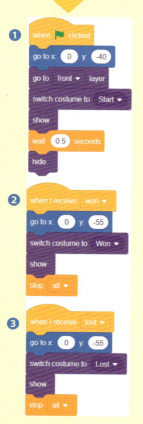

Then we add these three programs to show the costumes at the right time. Script ❶ shows the Start costume so the player has instructions at the start of the game. The `won` broadcast will make costume Won appear in script ❷, and the same happens for the Lost costume and `lost` broadcast in script ❸. The `stop all` block at the end of scripts ❷ and ❸ will stop the game.

STAGE 5

Don't forget to save your game before you take on the challenge to show off your soccer skills! Remember: Press the spacebar to kick the ball.

Scratchy's Challenge!!

Can you transform this into a shooting gallery game at an amusement park? How about making Pele a better goalkeeper? Give it a try!

SCRATCHY'S WILD RIDE

DESERT RALLY RACE

STAGE 6

Chapter Focus

Learn how to create a scrolling game, program complex movements for the sprites, and make a backdrop change over time.

Game

Control Scratchy's car to avoid obstacles and to run away from the Dark Minions in order to reach the Great Pyramid of Giza. Each time you crash your car, one of the Cosmic Defenders will jump out. If you crash your car four times, your car will break down!

Let's start by uploading a project called **06 – Desert Rally.sb2** (File ▶ Upload from your computer), which already has a bunch of sprites in it. It doesn't have any programs yet, but we'll add some soon.

First, let's look at the Stage. If you click the **Stage** to the right of the Sprite List, you can see that we have a lot of different backdrops.

Backdrops for the Stage are just like costumes for any other kind of sprite. So let's write a program that controls how they change.

Program ❶ will make the backdrop change over time in two loops, day and night. You can use the Duplicate tool to save time with the programming! This animation will give the Stage a cool look as Scratchy drives.

Program ❷ will make the Stage change its backdrop to the Win costume when the `finish` broadcast is received.

❶
```
when ⚑ clicked
forever
    repeat 8
        switch backdrop to Day_1
        wait 0.5 seconds
        switch backdrop to Day_2
        wait 0.5 seconds
        switch backdrop to Day_3
        wait 0.5 seconds
        switch backdrop to Day_4
        wait 0.5 seconds
    repeat 4
        switch backdrop to Night_1
        wait 0.5 seconds
        switch backdrop to Night_2
        wait 0.5 seconds
        switch backdrop to Night_3
        wait 0.5 seconds
        switch backdrop to Night_4
        wait 0.5 seconds
        switch backdrop to Night_5
        wait 0.5 seconds
        switch backdrop to Night_6
        wait 0.5 seconds
```

❷
```
when I receive finish
switch backdrop to Win
stop all
```

STAGE 6

We'll also have the Stage keep track of the time in program ❸. So create a variable called `Time` from the **Data** palette. We `set Time to 0` and then change it by 1 with each second. We'll use the `Time` variable again later.

Next, let's look at the road. Try to use the whole width of the Stage if you're drawing it!

Adding these programs to the **Road1** sprite will make it appear on the screen and scroll to the left.

①

Write program ① to make the `Scroll` variable continuously decrease by 1 (that is, `change Scroll by -1`).

②

Program ② will set the road's position. Set the y coordinate to 10 so it won't move up or down, and then add `set x to Scroll` in a `forever` loop. By doing this, the road will continuously move to the left as the `Scroll` variable changes.

③

Program ③ will make the `Scroll` variable reset to a 0 value once it reaches a value less than −479.

Tip: Why did we use the number −479? The width of the entire Scratch Stage is 480 pixels, so that's when it will roll off the Stage.

STAGE 6

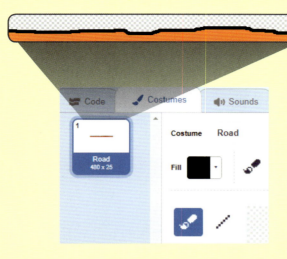

Now duplicate the Road1 sprite to create a second sprite called **Road2**.

Add this program to use the `Scroll` variable from the first road sprite. This time, we use a trick to make Road2 follow right behind Road1. By setting the x coordinate to `Scroll + 480`, we know Road2 will always follow behind Road1. This means that the player always has a road to drive on, no matter what!

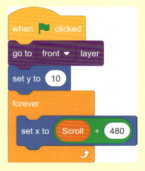

Next, switch to Scratchy's **Car** sprite.

Program **❶** for the Car does a lot of work. First, it sets the costume, size, and position.

The `forever` loop holds the rest of the program. The `change y by -5` block will pull the car down, giving it gravity. The `if touching color` block makes the car bounce up whenever it touches the black part of the road, making it seem like they're driving on a very bumpy road. The `if key up arrow pressed?` block will broadcast *jump* and then wait.

❶
```
when ⚑ clicked
switch costume to Car ▾
set size to 60 %
go to front ▾ layer
go to x: -150 y: -105
forever
    change y by -5
    if   touching color ● ?  and  y position < -105  then
        change y by 10
        wait 0.05 seconds
    if   key up arrow ▾ pressed?  then
        broadcast jump ▾ and wait
```

❷
```
when I receive jump ▾
repeat 15
    change y by 12
repeat until  touching color ● ?  and  y position < -105
    change y by -5
```

Program **❷** makes the car "listen" for the *jump* broadcast and makes the car jump up.

The `broadcast jump and wait` block in program **❶** will temporarily stop the first program so the second program can run.

STAGE 6

Now add program ❸ so that the car can move left and right.

In program ❹, we add some speech bubbles as instructions for the player.

In program ❺, we create a new variable called `Life`. When the `Life` value is less than 1, we'll set the car's costume to Boom! and then end the game with the `stop all` command.

Once you're finished with the Car sprite's programming, you can add some passengers—the Cosmic Defenders!

You can use the three sprites that are already in the project, or draw your own. I put **Gobo** at the back, **Fabu** in the middle, and **Pele** in the front. It's okay if your sprites overlap a bit—these guys are just coming along for the ride.

STAGE 6

Write this program for Gobo. It sets his size and position and uses the `go to` block so he'll always follow the Car sprite. Once the variable `Life` drops to less than 4 (`Life < 4`), he'll shoot to a random area. When he touches the top of the screen (`y position = 180`), we make him disappear by using the `hide` block.

Drag and copy Gobo's program onto Fabu in the Sprite List. You'll need to change only a few things. Most important, change the `repeat until` block to `Life < 3`, so Fabu will bounce out at a different time.

Do the same thing for Pele, but change the `Life` value to 2. Because Pele's sprite is a little bigger than the others, we also set his size to 25%.

STAGE 6

Now we can add the programming for the obstacles. First, let's take a look at the thorny and dangerous **Bush** sprite! It has two costumes.

And then write these three programs:

Program ❶ controls when the bush appears and makes sure it moves with the road. Once it touches the left edge of the screen, it'll disappear and switch to the next bush costume.

Program ❷ programs the Car to `change Life by -1` (that is, lose one life) whenever it touches an obstacle. Notice how we programmed the computer to check if the player still has enough Life value left using the `and` and `not` blocks.

And program ❸ makes the bush disappear once it receives the `finish` signal, which ends the game.

Now let's look at the **Tower** sprite, which also has two costumes. This obstacle will be tough to jump!

We can once again copy the program we created for the bushes. Edit the costume name and the time it appears, and you're good to go!

STAGE 6

Take a look at the sprite for **Legs**, the evil octopus Dark Minion. But don't you think it's a little boring just to have one image for him?

Why don't we try animating him?

In the Paint Editor, use the **Select** tool to grab the end of his tentacle.

Next, click this button to flip his arm up and then drag it back into place.

Do the same for his other tentacles, and there you go—a new look!

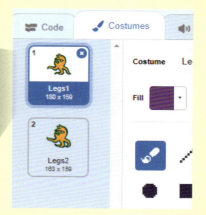

Tip: Editing existing costumes is an easy way to animate a character without having to redraw it. The Select and Rotate tools let you quickly change the position of a sprite's arms and legs.

Vector-based art is even easier to squish and squeeze into new shapes—this makes it great for animating characters.

Now let's get back to programming! Program ❶ makes Legs switch between his two costumes in a `forever` loop. Program ❷ makes him `hide` when he receives the `finish` broadcast.

STAGE 6

Programs ❸ and ❹ control Legs's movements and make him an unpredictable obstacle for Scratchy's car.

❸
```
when [flag] clicked
set size to (50) %
hide
forever
    wait (pick random (15) to (20)) seconds
    go to x: (230) y: (70)
    show
    repeat until <(x position) < (-230)>
        change x by (-3)
    end
    hide
end
```

❹
```
when [flag] clicked
forever
    repeat (10)
        change y by (-5)
        wait (0.05) seconds
    end
    repeat (10)
        change y by (5)
        wait (0.05) seconds
    end
end
```

Lastly, program ❺ for Legs adds a condition that will subtract life points from the **Life** variable, just as with the Bush and Tower obstacles.

❺
```
when [flag] clicked
wait (1) seconds
forever
    if <<touching (Car)?> and <not <(Life) = (0)>>> then
        change (Life) by (-1)
        wait (6) seconds
    end
end
```

And now we'll move on to the final sprite of the game: Egypt's Great Pyramid of Giza! Let's start with this photo:

By using this sprite, we'll make it look like Scratchy is "arriving" at the pyramids. I edited the Giza costume so that the cool backdrops will show through and so that the bottom matches the orange of the road. Now we can make the photo fit into our existing game.

Write a script so that the pyramid slowly appears from the right, after the game is run for 60 seconds. Once it reaches the center of the screen (`x position = 0`), it broadcasts the `finish` signal. When the other sprites receive this signal, the game ends.

STAGE 6

After saving your file, board Scratchy's speedy car and drive into the Sahara Desert to begin your wild adventure!

Scratchy's Challenge!!

Can you use these programs to create another scrolling game? Give it try! (Tip: The height of Scratch's screen is 360 pixels.) Make the game even more challenging by having the car go really fast!

THE LOST TREASURES OF GIZA

STAGE 7

ESCAPE THE MAZE!

STAGE 7

✚ Chapter Focus
Learn how to design an interactive maze with a guard, booby traps, and treasure!

🖉 Game
Guide Scratchy through the maze, and into the treasure room to collect the Magic Gem. After he picks up the Magic Gem, other traps in the pyramid are sprung, and he must escape!

For this game, begin by uploading a project file called **07 – The Maze.sb2** (File ▶ Upload from your computer). This project file has all the images you need for the game, but none of the sprites have any programs yet.

Take a look around, and especially take notice of the Stage. You can see that all of the walls in our maze have the same orange color. We'll use that color as the boundary, so Scratchy can't walk through walls!

STAGE 7

Click the sprite for Scratchy called **Indy-Cat** in the Sprite List. Then click the **Sounds** tab and add a sound effect for him. Either record a "meow" yourself or use the **Cat** sound effect. We'll write a program to make Scratchy meow whenever he bumps into a bad guy or trap.

Let's begin by thinking about how the game should start and how the player will win at the end of the game.

❶
```
when [flag] clicked
wait 0.5 seconds
say Get the gem and escape!! for 1 seconds
```

❷
```
when [flag] clicked
forever
  if <touching color [ ]?> then
    say Yeah!! for 1 seconds
    broadcast won and wait
```

Program ❶ gives the player the instructions for the game using the `say` block. Now when the game starts, the player will know he needs to grab the Magic Gem to win.

And, of course, to end the game, Scratchy needs to escape the maze with the Magic Gem. Now let's write a program for the end of the game. Program ❷ uses a special kind of block within a `forever` `if` loop. If Scratchy touches the color blue—that is, the blue sky of the exit door—he'll say "Yeah!!" and broadcast `won`, which will cause the game to end. (Because the maze itself doesn't have any blue, we don't have to worry about ending the game accidentally.)

To write program ❷, drag the `touching color` command from the **Sensing** palette into the `if` block. Click the color inside the block, and an eyedropper appears. Click the blue of the doorway, and you're all set. We'll use the `touching color` command for another neat programming trick next.

Now take a look at program **3**. It looks pretty complicated, but it's really not so hard. Can you tell what it does just by reading it?

First, we set the direction and position of Scratchy. That's simple enough. But what about the big `forever` loop? That holds all of the rest of the program, and that's how we'll program Scratchy's movements. First, if you press the up key, you can see there's a command that will `change y by 3`. But then *inside* that `if` loop, there's a second `if` loop!

If Scratchy is touching orange, the computer tells Scratchy to `change y by -3`. What's that all about? Well, did you notice that the walls of the maze are all orange? So if Scratchy bumps into the orange wall, we want the wall to stop him. And what does 3 + (–3) equal? That's right, 0. So when Scratchy touches the orange wall, he doesn't change his y position at all. He won't move! Cool.

The down, left, and right `if` loops work in just the same way, and they have a second `if` loop inside them as well. Make sure to pick orange with the eyedropper for every `if touching color` command.

Now Scratchy can't walk through the maze's walls or gates. Notice that the edge of the Stage has a thin band of orange, too. Scratchy can't walk off the Stage either! He's trapped in our maze, just like we want.

Finally, for program **4**, we use the `forever if` block and the `or` block to program what will happen whenever Scratchy bumps into a trap or a bad guy. A speech bubble will say "Oh!", the sound effect Cat will play, and Scratchy returns to his starting position.

Tip: The second `say` block is blank. This makes the "Oh!" disappear.

STAGE 7

Now is a good time to make sure that your programs work as you expected. Click 🏁, and make sure Scratchy moves up, down, left, and right. Try bumping into the walls of the maze. Does Scratchy stop moving once he hits a wall in all four directions? If not, go back and double-check your programming. (Remember that if Scratchy touches the orange wall, his movement should add up to 0.) Try hitting an obstacle or a bad guy to make sure Scratchy returns to the start of the maze.

Next, click the sprite for **Whiptail**, the Dark Minion guarding the pyramid. Write a program that sets his size and starting position and then makes him pace back and forth in the maze.

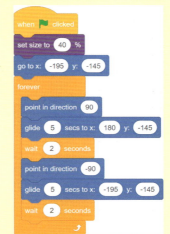

Then click the **Turnstile** sprite, and write a program to make it spin using the `turn` block. The sprite doesn't move around at all, so we just need to set one position.

At this point, take a look at the **Lock** and **Key** sprites, which are circled in blue below. Scratchy will need to pick up the Key first, in order to open the Lock. Let's create some programs for them next.

First, click the **Lock** in the Sprite List to give it a simple program—this just sets its location in the maze. The program that actually opens the gate is in the Key sprite.

STAGE 7

Tip: When creating the Key sprite, I used the **Set Costume Center** button in the Paint Editor to make sure Scratchy and the Key don't overlap.

Click the **Key** in the Sprite List, and listen to its sound in the **Sounds** tab. Then click the **Scripts** tab to write this program. We want a sound to play when Scratchy picks up the Key and then have the Key follow Scratchy, using the `go to` command. When the Key touches the Lock, the `gate open` signal is broadcast.

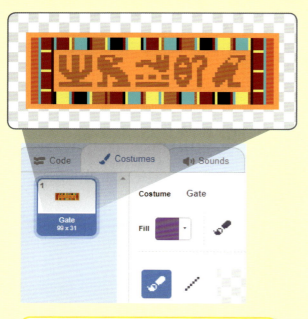

Now to program the **Gate** sprite. Because it has an orange border just like our maze, Scratchy can't enter the treasure room unless it moves!

Click the **Gate** in the Sprite List, and then test out the DirtyWhir sound to the Gate in its **Sounds** tab.

Now for some programs. Program ❶ just sets the Gate's location. Program ❷ makes the Gate glide out of the way when the gate open broadcast signal is received. Program ❸ plays a sound effect.

If you haven't tried out the game yet, give it a test now by clicking ⚑! See if you can get Scratchy to enter the treasure room.

STAGE 7

Next, let's program the **Magic Gem** sprite. We'll use a sound effect called Fairydust in the **Sounds** tab.

If it's not already there, you can just drag the sprite on top of its stand on the Stage.

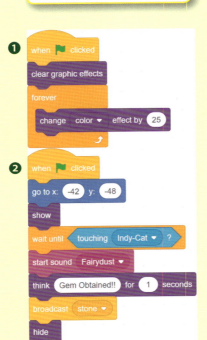

Then write two programs for it. Program ❶ makes the Magic Gem change colors. Program ❷ sets the Magic Gem's position and then uses a `wait until` block to determine what happens when Scratchy grabs the Magic Gem. When Scratchy touches the Magic Gem, it broadcasts stone. This will release the final traps in the maze!

When `stone` is broadcast, we want to activate the rolling stone and the spiked wall traps.

Our spiked wall trap will actually be two different sprites. **Wall_L** (the left side of the trap) gets one simple program to set its position.

STAGE 7

The right side has its own sprite called **Wall_R**. Create these two programs to set the position and make it move. This wall listens for the `stone` broadcast and begins to `glide` back and forth, most dangerously!

Waiting outside the passage is a rolling boulder sprite called **Stone**. I've used different shades of gray for the Stone to give it a 3D look.

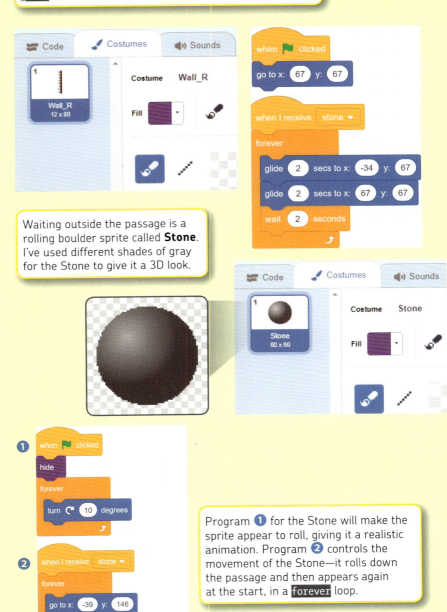

Program ❶ for the Stone will make the sprite appear to roll, giving it a realistic animation. Program ❷ controls the movement of the Stone—it rolls down the passage and then appears again at the start, in a `forever` loop.

Finally, we have a sprite for the winning screen called **You Won**.

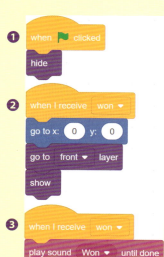

Write these three short programs. Program ❶ hides the sprite, and program ❷ displays it only when it receives won. Program ❸ plays the sound effect we added in the **Sounds** tab.

Tip: The `stop all` command in program ❸ will make the Stone, Whiptail, and all other sprites stop moving.

Wondering where that won broadcast will come from? Remember that Scratchy broadcasts won when he touches the blue in the doorway. We added that way back in program ❷ on page 108. So we're finished! Yes!

STAGE 7

Save your project so you don't lose any of your work! Now help Scratchy collect the Magic Gem and escape from the dangerous maze.

Scratchy's Challenge!!

By making the sprites smaller, you can create an even more complicated maze with more traps. Or you could add a second player and make it a race to the finish! Give it a try!

WIZARD'S RACE!

SORCERER'S CHALLENGE

STAGE 8

➕ Chapter Focus
Learn how to control the Stage with multiple costumes, play music with Scratch, and create other animations.

✏️ The Game
This is a simple "button-mashing" game. Rapidly press two keys back and forth to make Scratchy fly. He needs to beat all three levels within 15 seconds to collect the second Magic Gem.

Open the Scratch project **08 – Wizard's Race.sb2** (File ▶ Upload from your computer). This project file has all the sprites you'll need, but it doesn't have any programs yet. We can customize how it looks later. For now, we'll focus on the programming.

First, let's take a look at the Stage. It has three backdrops. We'll use these as levels for Scratchy's ride on the broomstick.

121

8 STAGE

Write program ❶ for the Stage to set its first backdrop. Program ❷ changes the Stage's backdrop when it receives the `next level` broadcast.

Tip: You'll need to choose **new message...** in the dropdown menu of the `when I receive` block to create the `next level` broadcast.

Create a `LEVEL` variable, and then write programs ❸ and ❹. Program ❸ makes sure that we start at level 1. Program ❹ listens for the `next level` broadcast from program ❹ on page 124 and increases the `LEVEL` variable by 1.

Create a second variable called `TIME`, and then write program ❺, which gives you 15 seconds to complete the race. Program ❻ broadcasts `lose` when you've run out of time.

Tip: Program ❻ has a couple tricky things in it. First, you'll need to create a new `start` broadcast in the `when I receive` block. The script also makes use of Scratch's built-in `timer` variable and uses some special commands from the **Operators**, **Events**, **Sensing**, and **Data** palettes. You need to use the `reset timer` block in program ❻, as Scratch's `timer` starts just as soon as you open the project. This command will let you try the game again after you've lost, too.

Next, we'll program the sprite for Scratchy the wizard. The sprite is called **Harry-Catter** and has two costumes. We'll give him two sound effects, too, in the **Sounds** tab.

Then write program ❶ to set his starting costume and position. Program ❷ makes him float up and down.

Program ❸ controls how Scratchy moves. The player will need to press the left and right arrow keys, one after another, to move Scratchy.

❸
```
when I receive start
forever
    if <key [left arrow ▼] pressed?> and <key [right arrow ▼] pressed?> then
        move (0) steps
    if <key [left arrow ▼] pressed?> and <not <key [right arrow ▼] pressed?>> then
        switch costume to [HarryCatter1 ▼]
        move (10) steps
        wait until <<key [right arrow ▼] pressed?> and <not <key [left arrow ▼] pressed?>>>
        switch costume to [HarryCatter2 ▼]
        move (10) steps
```

Can you see how this program works? The player can start with either the right or left arrow. The **not** block makes sure the player doesn't "cheat" by pressing both the right and left arrow keys at the same time.

❹
```
when I receive start
repeat (2)
    wait until <touching [Magic ▼]?>
    start sound [Fairydust ▼]
    start sound [Zoom ▼]
    broadcast [next level ▼]
    go to x: (-135) y: (65)
    say [Next Level!] for (0.5) seconds
say [Get the Magic Gem!] for (1) seconds
wait until <touching [Magic ▼]?>
broadcast [win ▼]
```

Finally, write program ❹ so that once Scratchy reaches the **Magic** sprite, sound effects will play, next level is broadcast, and Scratchy says "Next Level!" Remember that the next level broadcast will make the Stage change backdrops.

After that loop repeats twice, the player is on the third level. Scratchy will now say "Get the Magic Gem!" and broadcast win if he reaches the Magic sprite in time.

Now let's take a look at the costumes for Magic, the sprite that is our Magic Gate and the Magic Gem. The sprite will appear on the right of the Stage, and it will serve as Scratchy's goal for each of the three levels.

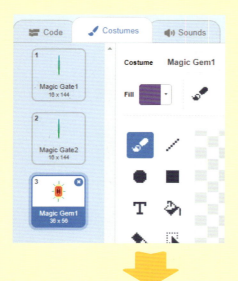

Here are those costumes for this sprite. We'll change costumes with each level, with the Magic Gem as Scratchy's goal for the third level. (That's why we have two Magic Gate costumes and one Magic Gem costume—we have three levels.)

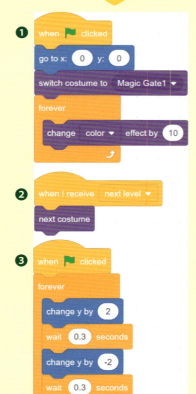

Program ❶ sets the sprite's position and its first costume and creates a `change color` animation. Program ❷ changes the costume with each `next level` broadcast, and program ❸ makes the sprite float up and down.

Now we can add some magical visual effects to our game. There is a sprite called **Terrain** that has these three costumes.

Next, write program ❶ to continuously change the Terrain sprite's costumes and set its starting position. This gives a neat animated effect to the ground. Program ❷ makes the Terrain change colors magically!

STAGE 8

Now it's time for the text for our game. The **Titles** sprite has a bunch of instructions for the player. We'll use its Countdown_3, Countdown_2, Countdown_1, and Go costumes to create a countdown to start this race!

Hit L & R keys to fly through 3 levels within 15 seconds!!

Ready?

3 2

1 GO!!

You Win!! You Lose!!

The Titles sprite has three sounds. You can add your own in the **Sounds** tab.

❶ Write program ❶ to set the order of each costume. We use the `play note` and `play sound` blocks to add fun noises to the game.

Here's that `start` broadcast at long last. Remember that this is what the Stage and Scratchy are waiting for!

Finally, write programs ❷ and ❸ for the winning and losing screens, depending on whether the Titles sprite receives the `win` or `lose` broadcast. And now our game is complete!

STAGE 8

Save your project, and get ready for a race! Click 🏁, put your fingers on the keys, and get ready to set a speed record.

Scratchy's Challenge!!

Can you edit this game to make it a two-player race? How about a two-person watermelon-eating contest? Give it a try!

THE FINAL FIGHT... IN DARK SPACE

STAGE 9

THE FINAL FIGHT

STAGE 9

 Chapter Focus

Learn how to design a *fighting game*. We'll create two characters with unique fight moves, custom health counters, and more. To make custom animations for Scratchy's three fight moves, we'll use a special trick to swap between four different sprites.

 The Game

Take control of Scratchy for the final fight with the Dark Wizard. Use his saber spin, saber throw, and force attack to defeat the Dark Wizard.

Here's a look at the final game we'll create. You'll need to jump over the Dark Wizard's dangerous fireballs and launch a counterattack!

This sprite represents the Dark Wizard's health.

This sprite represents Scratchy's health.

The computer controls the Dark Wizard.

The player controls Scratchy.

Let's start by uploading a blank project called **09 - Final Fight.sb2** (File ▸ Upload from your computer). This project has all the sprites we'll need, even the Stage. Now let's move on to the exciting stuff—programming!

STAGE 9

Let's take a look at the **Cat** sprite. We'll use the first four costumes at the start of the game to make the saber look like it's extending! There's also a fifth costume we'll use for Scratchy's jump animation.

Make sure you click the correct cat sprite in the Sprite List—it's the one named **Cat**. This game has a few different sprites for Scratchy! You'll see why soon.

I also added three sound effects to this sprite's **Sounds** tab. Don't forget that you can record your own!

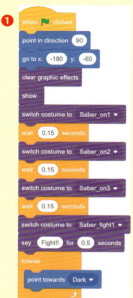

① Write program ①, which will make a cool starting animation for the game. First, we put Scratchy where he needs to go. Then we use `switch costume to` blocks to change among his three costumes. Next, we use the `say` block to tell Scratchy to say "Fight!" Finally, we use the `point towards` block in a `forever` loop to make Scratchy always face his enemy, the Dark Wizard.

Next, we'll write programs ②, ③, and ④ so that we can move Scratchy to the left and right.

Try clicking 🚩 to make sure all your programs work as expected. The game won't really work yet, but you should be able to move Scratchy back and forth.

Programs ⑤, ⑥, and ⑦ are for Scratchy's jump ability. Program ⑤ animates the jump by switching costumes, broadcasts jump to control programs ⑥ and ⑦, and also creates "gravity" in the `change y by -10` block. When Scratchy lands, he changes back to his original saber fight costume. In program ⑥, we determine how high Scratchy can jump. Program ⑦ is just a sound effect for the jump.

Tip: Notice how we used the `broadcast and wait` block in program ②. That's to make sure the player doesn't jump too often or jump right off the screen! Scratchy must reach y position -60 to jump again. That's the platform's height.

STAGE 9

Now let's use some new broadcasts to make Scratchy's fight moves! We'll use a cool trick. Whenever Scratchy uses a fight move, he'll actually change into a new sprit. Each fight move will get its own sprite, as you'll see.

So we'll hide the Cat sprite and broadcast a unique signal for each move—attack1, attack2, and attack3—in program ❽.

Programs ❾, ❿, and ⓫ use broadcasts called show1, show2, and show3. We'll use these broadcasts at the end of each attack sequence. These will make Scratchy show up again on the screen. The hide and show blocks are like partners—one makes a sprite disappear, and the other makes it reappear.

Next, create a new variable using the **Data** palette, and name it HP (for Health Points). Write program ⓬ to determine Scratch's starting HP and how dangerous the Dark Wizard's attacks are. Every time Scratchy touches the Dark sprite or Fireball sprite, he loses 5 HP and plays the Hurt sound, and the change color effect block animates him.

The last program, ⓭, determines what happens when all of Scratchy's HP is gone: A broadcast called lose is sent.

Now let's set up some costumes for Scratchy's attacks. But instead of adding even more costumes to the Cat sprite, we'll use a new sprite, called **Saber Spin**, for the spinning saber attack. (Remember how we made a program to hide the Cat sprite in program ❽ on the previous page?)

Then give a listen to the **Spin** sound effect in the **Sounds** tab.

STAGE 9

Next, use these four programs to control the saber spin attack. Program ❶ makes this sprite `go to` the location of the original Cat sprite. Program ❷ is just a sound effect when the sprite receives `attack1`.

Program ❸ makes the light saber swirl around three times—by using the block `next costume` in a `repeat 36` loop—and then broadcasts `show1` to tell the Cat sprite that the attack move is finished.

Program ❹ determines how much damage the saber does to the Dark Wizard's `Dark HP` variable.

We'll use that `Dark HP` variable to keep track of the Dark Wizard's health. Recall that Scratchy already has his health variable, called `HP`. Take a moment to create `Dark HP` in the **Data** palette now—we'll need to use this variable in all three of Scratchy's attacks!

To give our program a cool look, we can add a ring around the saber, with the **Ring** sprite.

Tip: To make sure the Ring shows up in the right place during the game, move the Ring so that the costume lines up with Scratchy's hand.

138

❶ Then write some simple programs for the Ring. Program ❶ makes the Ring appear in the right place, and programs ❷ and ❸ make sure that the Ring appears only during the attack1 sequence. The fisheye effect in program ❹ makes the Ring expand and contract in a cool animation.

❷

❸ We'll give all of Scratchy's attacks some major defensive power by skipping the health (HP) programming. (Remember that after the end of the saber spin attack, the script broadcasts show1, which shows the original Cat sprite, which is vulnerable to attack! This defensive power is only temporary.)

❹

Let's check our work. Click 🏁 and make sure that pressing 1 activates the saber spin attack! You can test each fight move as you finish its programs.

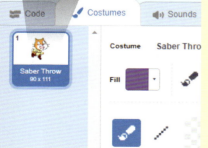

Next, let's look at the sprite for the second fight move—the saber throw attack. It's a simple sprite with just one costume. We'll write some programs for it to make sure this sprite faces the right way and listens for the broadcast attack2 to start (and the broadcast show2 to hide).

STAGE 9

The cool part of this attack is actually throwing the saber. We'll give it a second sprite, called **Thrown Saber**, just like we added a second sprite (the Ring) for the saber spin attack. The Thrown Saber sprite has four costumes: a simple saber, followed by three explosion animations.

We'll add a program to use these explosion costumes when we hit the Dark Wizard.

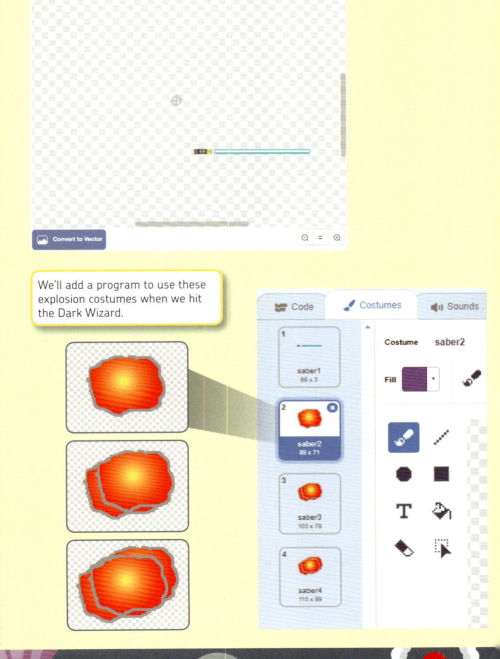

You can use a sound effect for the Thrown Saber and then write program ❶ to make it play. Program ❷ determines how much damage the saber throw attack does.

❶
```
when I receive attack2
play sound Saber Throw until done
```

❷
```
when ⚑ clicked
forever
    if <touching Dark?> then
        change Dark HP by -100
        wait 1 seconds
```

❸
```
when ⚑ clicked
hide
```

❹
```
when I receive attack2
go to Cat
point towards Dark
switch costume to saber1
go to front layer
show
wait 0.2 seconds
glide 0.5 secs to x: x position of Dark y: y position of Dark
if <touching Dark?> then
    switch costume to saber2
    wait 0.1 seconds
    switch costume to saber3
    wait 0.1 seconds
    switch costume to saber4
    wait 0.1 seconds
    hide
    broadcast show2 and wait
else
    wait 0.3 seconds
    hide
    broadcast show2 and wait
```

Then write these programs. Program ❸ hides the flying saber until we need it. Program ❹ points the saber at the Dark Wizard and launches it! When it hits the Dark sprite, we make the sprite switch to its explosion costumes. Note the special `glide` command that finds the Dark Wizard, no matter where he is. At the end of this program, we broadcast `show2`. This will make Scratchy switch back to his original Cat sprite.

No matter where he goes, we can hit the Dark Wizard with the saber throw attack—pretty powerful! Give this attack move a test, too, and make sure it hits the Dark Wizard. Press 2 after clicking ⚑.

141

STAGE 9

Now let's program the final fight move, the **Force Attack**. Don't forget you can add a new sound effect for it in the **Sounds** tab.

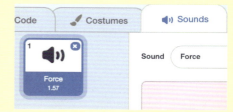

Program ❶ hides this costume until we launch the force attack. Program ❷ uses the ghost effect to make the lights flash. Even though our sprite has only one costume, we created a cool effect—this program will make our attack pulse with energy!

Write program ❸ to play your sound effect, and program ❹ to make sure this attack will reduce `Dark HP` by 100 if the Force Attack sprite touches the Dark Wizard.

The final program ⑤ will help Scratchy to land when he uses this attack while jumping.

Now Scratchy has all three of his fight moves. Click 🏁, and test your program to make sure it behaves exactly as you expected! Walk around; press 1, 2, and 3 to activate the fight moves; and try jumping around the screen. Now Scratchy is ready for this fight.

Finally, we can get to the Dark Wizard!

First, let's set his starting position (x: 170, y: -30) and his size (65% of the original sprite, so he's not too big) in program ❶. Program ❷ controls how he moves on the platform. He just picks a random spot between x:-85 and x:170 and glides there in a `forever` loop.

In program ❸, we use the `Dark HP` variable we created earlier to keep track of the Dark Wizard's health. This program also makes sure he always faces his enemy, Scratchy.

In program ❹, we add two sets of `if` blocks inside a `forever` command. If the Dark Wizard touches one of Scratchy's attacks, he'll `change color`. (Scratchy's attacks already have programs that subtract from the variable `Dark HP`.)

Now for the Dark Wizard's furious fireball attack! This is a new sprite called **Fireball**, and you can add a sound effect for it, too.

Write program ❶ to give it a sweet animated look using a `fisheye` effect.

Then write program ❷ to control how often the Dark Wizard uses his attack and where the fireball goes once it's launched! Can you see how it works?

Program ❸ plays our sound effect for the Fireball.

Tip: We used `move` instead of `glide` so that Scratchy has a chance to jump away. The `if touching Cat` and `if touching edge` statements make the fireball disappear once it touches Scratchy or the edge of the screen.

The `wait 0.25 secs` block in the `if touching Cat` loop makes sure that the fireball actually does damage before disappearing!

Don't forget to double-check your programming by making sure that these fireballs do damage, too. Click 🏁 and let one of the fireballs hit Scratchy! Ouch!

STAGE 9

Now that the main programming is finished, let's add custom HP counters for each character, just like you'd see in any other fighting game. First, let's use the yellow bar sprite for Scratchy called **Health**.

Write this program to make the health bar become smaller each time HP is subtracted, using the `set size` block. If Scratchy's HP goes lower than 21%, the bar will change color as a warning to the player. The final `if` loop hides this sprite if HP is completely depleted.

I put a sprite on top of the Health sprite called **Health Box**. The bottom half of the Health Box is transparent, which lets a triangular portion of the health bar show through. The Health Box gets a short program just to set its position.

To hide the variable HP so it doesn't appear on the screen, just uncheck the HP variable in the **Data** palette. There's also a `hide variable` command, if you want to add it to your programs.

Now we can see how much HP Scratchy has left, just by looking at the top-left corner of the Stage.

STAGE 9

For the Dark Wizard's HP meter, we'll use a costume-switching program. The **Dark HP** sprite has seven costumes.

After taking a look at the Dark HP costumes, add this program. It sets the size, position, and conditions of the `Dark HP` variable when the sprite changes costumes.

148

Next, go to the Stage and find the Dark HP variable in the top-right corner. You can take your pick from one of three looks (just double-click to change it):

- Standard view
- Adjustable view (click and drag the ball to change a variable's value)
- Numeric view

Because we have a custom sprite, let's use the simplest view, the numeric one, to display the Dark HP variable.

Now take a look at the sprites for the winning screen (**Win**) and the losing screen (**Lose**). The winning screen gets the two programs below and shows itself only when it receives the win broadcast from the Dark Wizard sprite, once he's out of Dark HP.

The losing screen has two really similar programs. Now we're finished!

STAGE 9

After saving your work, give the game a try. You'll definitely want to play this one full screen. Step into Scratchy's shoes for the final battle.

Scratchy's Challenge!!

Feel like playing the bad guy instead? Just program some movement controls for the Dark Wizard, and you'll have a two-player game. You can even add more fight moves! Give it a try!

EPILOGUE

10 STAGE

STAGE 10

CREDITS

STORY AND GAME PROGRAMMING

EDMOND KIM PING HUI
THE LEAD PROJECT
THE HONG KONG FEDERATION OF YOUTH GROUPS

ARTWORK

LOL DESIGN LTD.

SCRATCH SOFTWARE

MITCHEL RESNICK
MIT MEDIA LAB'S LIFELONG KINDERGARTEN GROUP

ENGLISH EDITION

NO STARCH PRESS

THANKS FOR PLAYING!

CLOSING THOUGHTS

I hope you've enjoyed the story of Mitch and Scratchy's adventure, and their success in defeating the Dark Wizard with their kindness. I hope you've also experienced the power of hands-on learning with Scratch. Designing games is one of the best ways to learn to program.

But there is no single way to learn about technology. As long as you have the spirit to take risks, learn from failure, stand by your goals, and strive to excel, you will be able to learn a great deal. And Scratch is an excellent tool for learning in such a practical fashion.

I sincerely hope that this book will encourage you to create Scratch projects that surprise and delight your families and friends!

Edmond Kim Ping Hui
Team Leader and Registered Social Worker (HK)
Learning through Engineering, Art, and Design Project
The Hong Kong Federation of Youth Groups

ONLINE RESOURCES

Visit *http://nostarch.com/superscratch3/* and download the Resources file. When you unzip the file, you'll find:

Scratch projects The projects from the book, which you can play, build on, remix, and reimagine! Don't forget that you can use these sprites, scripts, and sound effects in your very own games. Just drag them into your Backpack (see page 39).

"Getting Started with Scratch" A short guide to key Scratch concepts written by Scratch's creators at MIT.

The Scratch Project also offers many resources.

1 SCRATCH—IMAGINE, PROGRAM, SHARE

http://scratch.mit.edu/

This is the official website of Scratch. Here, you can browse, play, and remix over a million different Scratch projects from around the world!

PLAYABLE GAMES ON THE SCRATCH WEBSITE 2

http://scratch.mit.edu/users/nostarch/

This web page contains all of the projects listed in this book. Comments are welcome, and you can easily download these projects to redesign them however you want!

SCRATCH WIKI
https://en.scratch-wiki.info/

Scratch users have created a wiki that contains a lot of interesting content and articles.

SCRATCH FORUMS
https://scratch.mit.edu/discuss/

A forum for Scratchers to share ideas and ask and answer questions.

SCRATCHED
http://scratched.gse.harvard.edu/

An information-sharing website created for teachers and other educators who use Scratch. Share your success stories, exchange Scratch resources, ask questions, and more.

LIFELONG KINDERGARTEN GROUP AT MIT'S MEDIA LAB
https://www.media.mit.edu/groups/lifelong-kindergarten/overview/

This is the birthplace of Scratch—the official homepage for MIT Media Lab's Lifelong Kindergarten Group. You can learn more about Professor Mitchel Resnick (the creator of Scratch), and about other creative education and design tools.

MORE BOOKS FROM no starch press

PYTHON FOR KIDS
A PLAYFUL INTRODUCTION TO PROGRAMMING

by JASON R. BRIGGS
DEC 2012, 344 PP., $29.95, *full color*
ISBN 978-1-59327-407-8

MAKE YOUR OWN TWINE GAMES!

by ANNA ANTHROPY
MAY 2019, 104 PP., $17.95, *full color*
ISBN 978-1-59327-938-7

THE LEGO® BOOST ACTIVITY BOOK
A BEGINNER'S GUIDE TO ROBOTICS

by DANIELE BENEDETTELLI
NOV 2018, 272 PP., $24.95, *full color*
ISBN 978-1-59327-932-5

LEARN ROBOTICS WITH RASPBERRY PI
BUILD AND CODE YOUR OWN MOVING, SENSING, THINKING ROBOTS

by MATT TIMMONS-BROWN
JAN 2019, 240 PP., $24.95, *full color*
ISBN 978-1-59327-920-2

MISSION PYTHON
CODE A SPACE ADVENTURE GAME!

by SEAN MCMANUS
OCT 2018, 280 PP., $29.95, *full color*
ISBN 978-1-59327-857-1

UPDATES

Visit *https://nostarch.com/superscratch3*
for updates, errata, and other information.

Super Scratch Programming Adventure! is set in Chevin, CCMeanwhile, Century Schoolbook, House-A-Rama Kingpin (© House Industries), The Sans Mono Condensed, and Kozuka Gothic Pro.